A National Service C

Written by David W. Overy

Copyright 2017

Contact: rafdigby@gmail.com

Front cover:
De Havilland Vampire, 11 Squadron

Back cover:
David with De Havilland Tiger Moth, RAF Digby, 1951

1

David took great pleasure in keeping records throughout his life and when he died in 2017 the family were fascinated to find this "NATIONAL SERVICE ODYSSEY' among his papers and we felt he would have liked to share his experiences with others, especially during this centenary year of the RAF. We do hope you will find it an interesting read.

Prologue

This is a story, over half a century old, of one of many teenagers, who were drafted into the Services. It was an adventure that ended soon after his 20th birthday as abruptly as it had begun. National Service was, initially, a traumatic episode in the life of many of those who experienced conscription. We were unused to being away from home and certainly not prepared for the shock tactics which would be employed against us to rouse us from our comfortable lifestyle to try and weld us into a cohesive battle force.

After I had written this tale, I came across on the Internet, a similar narrative written by another National Service recruit. He was not quite a contemporary, as it appears his call-up was some 6-8 months ahead of me, and our paths diverted after the initial training. He went to serve in a trade as an ordinary airman while I passed into the aircrew training phase and was subsequently commissioned. Nevertheless, much of what he tells corroborates my own recollections of the induction and initial training. He does make very interesting additional comments on the social scene in the early 1950's and has also recorded the then current international political situation, something that I did not tackle, which resulted in the period of National Service being extended. This is my story.

For most of us life at the start of the second half of the century was family orientated. Just 6 years after the end of the second world war, it was a time of austerity. Most of the population earned just enough to live on, possessions were few in number and treasured, certainly not amassed. Consumer goods generally were not available or very limited in choice, packaged foreign holidays were not only unheard of but travel abroad was beyond the reach, and in any case holidays with pay had not yet been introduced for many workers. For the lucky ones a week in a boarding house at a UK seaside resort was the usual annual holiday and for most of those working in the factories in the north and elsewhere it meant being regimented into "Wakes Weeks" - at a fixed time in the summer when whole factories closed for maintenance. During the war "Holidays at Home" had been the theme and that continued to suffice for many as did the alternative of staying with relatives. The aim in life for most youngsters was to get a good job with prospects and security, to find a compatible mate, save for a couple of years and get engaged and, from that joint pledge, save a lot more to raise enough to marry, leave home and set up a family. From it a new young family would spring up and one could take pride in the achievement of having done it.

From this family idyll, by law, every male of 18 years was to be plucked away from home and trained to kill other human beings. The legislation was called The National Service Acts and included every male fit to serve and not exempted for a period of study. At school I had intended to go to London University as I had matriculated but thought that I might as well get national service over before starting higher education rather than be swept into it as soon as I graduated as exemption would only have lasted until graduation day. So I left school to start a career in the business world - and to raise much needed cash in the 2 intervening years! However, I made a big mistake in my planning. Unknown to me, because my grammar school at Varndean failed to advise me of it, there was a time limit to registering my matriculation exemption with the university. On leaving the service, my enquiry about late entry revealed that I had missed the deadline. I might have been given dispensation after the years of study to be a pilot. However, the anticipated restrictions of academic life following the adrenaline flowing activities of the last two years, a total loss of income while at university and having to study with a lot of young kids with no life experience (!) all decided me to pursue professional studies in my own time. However, it is interesting to compare the attitude of London University to that of Trinity College Cambridge as experienced by author Brian Thompson. Writing in his book "Clever Girl", he relates that having been made to do National Service by his father rather than being allowed to stay on at 6th form to take the open examination he wrote direct to Trinity for a place. He even wrote on NAFFI notepaper! They not only offered him a place but agreed to waive all entry formalities. Had London been more forthcoming I might have taken up a place.

The odd thing about my being accepted for

flying training was the fact that I had never been up in an aeroplane, unlike many of the companions I was about to meet on the journey. Most had been in the ATC and at least had been up in a glider, some had actually experienced powered flight particularly those with some experience in University Air Squadrons. My experience at school had been in the Combined Cadet Force (CCF) very much infantry based with my feet firmly on the ground.

Nevertheless, despite no previous experience I was about to embark upon a long journey. It would not be true to say that I had had no interest in flight. I remember having on my wall a coloured pull-out from a magazine describing the history of flight starting with the ill-fated attempt by Icarus. My Saville-Sneath penguins from 1941 record all the aircraft operating at wartime and were heavily used. Particularly, I made a large number of balsa wood gliders the most successful based on the Gotha. Perhaps it was predestined that the Gotha glider was a twin boom machine and that I would one day fly twin-boomed fighter aircraft. For the 1942 Christmas a visiting "aunt" tried to dissuade me from wanting "Flight Today" rather than a child's book as a Christmas present- this volume is still in our library. I remember also a kit of a Boulton & Paul Defiant that dad (mostly) helped me make up although its weight defied all attempts to have it fly as the rubber band propulsion was totally inadequate! Also, still in my possession, is a Meccano model of a Tiger Moth, with a revolving propeller, which was regularly assembled and taken to bits. I also spent time staying in London with cousin Alan during the WWII and in the Battle of Britain had witnessed the dog-fights and a parachute landing in the allotments close by - unfortunately it was one of ours that had been knocked out!

And so it was that in July 1951 that the process of law led me like a lamb to slaughter.

Chapter Two

The Call-Up

A summons dated 12 July 1951 required me to attend Oddfellows Hall in Queens Road, Brighton on 19 July for a medical and registration. The form stated that 14 days notice would subsequently be given of call-up. At the registration we had to state a preference for type of work we expected to do or trade we would like to follow. I wanted to follow dad into the Royal Navy but I was told that the Service was not recruiting. So I opted for flying or tank commander, both of which were ridiculed by the overbearing Sgt Major on duty but I stuck to my guns and insisted that he put me down for aircrew. On page 10 of Les Hunt's account of National Service he makes reference to the options available to him on recruitment. Call-up was on 28th August.

Chapter Three

Royal Air Force Initiation
RAF Padgate

I have no record of the process by which I was drawn into the vast machine for turning raw civilians into servicemen but, imprinted on the memory, much of it is still vivid after 60 years. Perhaps that is because of the monotony, the banality of the procedures and seemingly time wasting activities in those early reception days.

On 28 August, 1951, having obviously received my call-up papers which I presume would have included a one-way rail warrant to Warrington station in Cheshire. Dad with Mum drove me to catch the train from Brighton station. It was a Tuesday which, unbeknown to me, was the day that all aspiring aircrew recruits made the journey. I was heading for No.1 Reception Unit, RAF Padgate to where many of the National Service recruits reported. Those unlucky ones who did not make the grade for aircrew would stay to complete 8 weeks "square bashing" before being allocated a posting to the trade for which they were destined. There were other Initial Training camps but I cannot now remember where, most being somewhere in the north of England.

We had been required to take with us a bag of some sort to hold a few personal possessions and to accommodate civilian clothes once kitted out in Air Force blue. For the purpose I had bought a small brown suitcase of the compressed board type - and which I still have - and had proudly painted on my initials in black. At this time (1951) one did not have much experience of long train travel because of the restrictions which applied both during and after the war. However, somehow I made my way across London and boarded the designated train and spent the intervening time watching through the window. Down the corridor a noisy lot of East-Enders were busy at cards and the train was very full as so many people were in uniform at that time. In my carriage was an army sergeant with his wife and their baby, returning from an overseas posting, and at one stage in the journey we were all asked to leave the compartment while his wife breast-fed the infant. And to make sure we could not see from the corridor, he obscured the windows with his uniform greatcoat!

At Warrington we were met by a crowd of NCOs, barking instructions as we were hassled into the transports. These vehicles comprised the ubiquitous military version Bedford lorries in Air Force light blue with a canvas tilt over and a row of lightly padded bench seats either side facing inwards and a double row down the centre. The tailboard dropped to provide a toehold to clamber up into the vehicle. Most of us were unused to this manoeuvre (but which we would become skilled at!) which gave the junior NCOs their sport at screaming at our heels for faster movement.

We were then moved off to our new "home" experiencing another of the delights of military service in the "other ranks" - a ride in a Bedford. This vehicle was the standard Services troop transporter being a basic lorry, fitted with the benches and a canvass tilt. The driver's jerkiness combined with the hardness of the skimpy seating did not make for the most comfortable of rides, but again we would get used to it.

Our first sight of the camp was looking rearward as the canvas flaps at the tailgate were pulled aside and we had a fleeting glimpse of the immaculate guardhouse and its spick and span occupants at the barrier. At the entrance by the main gate, as every station would have had at that time, an obsolete Spitfire or Hurricane was tethered.

I vaguely remember an induction procedure where we confirmed personal details for the record, were allocated our service number (with admonishment to memorise it immediately for failure to quote it would result in a "charge"), given a medical and required to sign the Official Secrets Act. 2528532 A/c2 Overy DW was now an official member of His Majesty's (i.e. King George VI) armed services. Having travelled long and far we must have been given a meal on arrival but without "irons" (see below) I am not sure how we ate it. Probably immediately after registration we would have been sent off into huts.

The service hut is an institution in its own right being a long single-storey wooden structure with a door at one end. Immediately on the right of the door is a bedroom for the corporal in charge of the hut. Down the middle of the hut are two cast iron circular pipe stoves to provide heat. Folding tables with chairs stand between them and down either side of the hut under the windows is a row of 15 metal beds with a locker alongside completing the furnishings. The lockers are lockable but no lock is provided and so the NAFFI enjoyed quite a nice sale of a cheap standard pattern padlock - and probably all the keys were the same! The Corporal is the one person who will now control your life during the sojourn at Padgate. He will either tell you what to do or give permission for you to do it but no other action would be possible. There is an axiom in the training camps, "If it moves salute it, if it does not move paint it white"! The stock of coal outside each hut at the Padgate initial training (square-bashing) camp proper actually was painted white! It was said that fuel was never used in the stoves to avoid too much cleaning in the hut and to keep the polish on the stove for bull night. So it is likely that on our first night we were marched to the airmen's mess and the temporary loan of irons was authorised. From here we would have been marched to the bedding store to draw bedding - if I remember correctly 2 blankets and two flannel sheets. Some of the latter were too small to fit the bed - we later learned that it was not unusual for them to be torn in half by those running the bedding store to cover up deficiencies - everything had a resale value!

On the next day the parade for the issue of clothing was amazing to behold - if one were not actually engaged in the mad scramble. Each item of uniform, which more or less might fit, was thrust at you as you shuffled along in line. Then you moved to a long table where thoroughly bored airmen set up large rubber stamps with your personal service number and proceeded to stamp each item with indelible ink. Numbers went everywhere and anywhere on each garment as no precision was applied to the stamping. It was even done over creases! When it came to brushes, "irons" (knife, fork & spoon) and the brass button cleaner the numbers were hammered in using large dies - "2528532" can still be made out on brushes which we use in our shoe cleaning kit.

Deficiency chits were issued for any item out of stock, including any articles of clothing which could not be made to fit - all the "housewives" (sewing kits) were out of stock. One never caught up with me for my entire service. These chits had to be guarded like gold dust because at the frequent kit inspections they were absolution from anything not displayed. Replacements for anything lost would have to be paid for - as well as being put on a "charge" for not displaying a complete kit.

Fitted in between all this activity was a visit to the camp barber. I thought I had had my hair cut short just before I went in, but it did not pass muster and like lambs we all were sent to be shorn - at our own expense!

One of the remarkable procedures, 3 times a day, was the march to the mess hall. We were

13

formed up by our hut corporal and marched down to eat the appropriate meal of the day. When finished we formed up to march back again but this incorporated the ritual of the cleansing of irons. Outside of the mess huts were long troughs of hot water and we trailed our knife, fork and spoon and the mug through the hot water they contained (complete with greasy scum on the surface) until at the end, hopefully, they were sufficiently clean to reuse. Both going and returning the "irons" and mug had to be held a certain way in the left hand with the knuckles in the small of the back. We would be marching in double file while the corporal droned out the mantra - 'Eft, 'Eft, ... 'Eft, Right, Left in slow time.

Our days were spent on the parade ground and forming up into sections with Corporal Garrity in charge, probably the thickest NCO in the Royal Air Force. Having come together as a full parade we would then be divided up into sub groups such as "those with deficiency chits for boots fall out and reform to one side". And so it went on until we were spread all over the parade ground in little groups, mindless time wasting until it was time for the NAFFI break - usually tea and a wad from the mobile canteen - if you could afford it. Parade would then reform and it was drill until lunchtime. Some of those on parade would still be wearing their own sports jackets over serge trousers because their special size of battledress had not arrived from the tailors.

The NAFFI was a place of solace for some, particularly those who could not stomach the camp food. If they could get away from the hut they eked out their 4/- a day pay on NAFFI canteen food (in my opinion no better but at least it was chips with everything).

In the evenings we were introduced to hut bull night when everything in the hut had to be scrubbed, cleaned and polished exceptionally well. On top of hut cleaning, attending to our personal kit - the daily routine of cleaning and polishing boots and buttons and blanco'ing webbing took more time. There was quite a lot of webbing to be treated, blue for everyday use but when there was a special parade, like the one at Lincoln cathedral (see below) then all the blue had to be got off and replaced by white. The special button gadget was to ensure that no metal polish was transferred to the serge of the uniform. My button polisher has become lost over time but we still have one from Betty's dad's army days.

A lot of time was spent floor polishing and a great heavy device on a pole (known as a bumper) was constantly drawn across the service to maintain the shine. So that we did not scratch the pristine surface of the floor, once it had been polished, we were expected to shuffle from the door to our bedspace and back on pads of felt stacked by the door.

Our huts lie between the camp entrance and the mess. Beyond were the huts of the permanent camp for those undertaking their ordeal of square-bashing. Overlooking the huts was the grim shadow of the massive water tower. About once a week one of the poor devils who could no longer stand the torment climbed to the top and several suicides occurred of those who succeeded in throwing themselves off.

One of the amusements was to see the new day's arrivals saluting the head of camp entertainment who, being an ENSA civilian, had a sort of uniform. Nobody, among the newest recruits, following the principle above, took any chances!

Fortunately the tedium was broken for me by our departure to RAF Hornchurch.

Chapter Four

Aircrew Selection Centre, RAF Hornchurch.

I have no record and very little recollection of travelling to the Aircrew Selection unit at RAF Hornchurch in Essex. We travelled from Warrington to London and on by train from Liverpool Street Station. I think we were there for 2 or 3 days as the rigorous testing was carried out on reactions and co-ordination. We had all sorts of puzzles to solve, by shape, colour or design, odd shapes that were out of order to turn round, all that sort of thing, against a stop watch. One mechanical device required us to use a rudder bar and hand controls and react correctly to various images and crash down on other buttons when red or green lights flashed. There were pages of written intelligence tests, interviews and a very thorough medical examination. In the course of completing one questionnaire we had to state our preferences for the five aircrew categories: from pilot, flight engineer, air gunner, wireless operator or navigator. That was the order I had entered because I thought that navigating would be boring, stuck with the head down all the while the rest of the crew were looking out of the window! The final interview was conducted and I was invited to sit down and "take off my bonnet". Funny how some things like that phrase stick in the mind. The officer could not understand my dislike of navigating and finally said that he would change its order on my form to second preference. I later learned that I had passed out for aircrew training but, disappointingly, would be graded as cadet *navigator.* To this day I do not know why but probably they were getting short of trainee navigators and my maths results were good. But it was heartbreak for many who had come with us - either they failed on the dexterity tests or the written papers or worse, the exacting medical or for reasons of colour blindness. For them it was back to Padgate and absorption into the AC2 square-bashing units.

All too soon we were back on the train to Warrington, and for some of us, with lighter hearts that we had accomplished one more step on the journey.

Chapter Five

No 1 Reception Unit
RAF Padgate

Back at Padgate we were now officially aircrew cadets and were given a white disc to wear under our airman's cap badge. We had to suffer more of Garrity's parades but since most of the kit deficiencies had now been resolved his brain could not think of any other way of dividing us up on the parade ground so it was mostly pure drill; but another mental torture interposed. Apart from drill in the first part of the morning and the afternoon, we filled in the rest of the day with mind-numbing activities such us digging daisies out of the grass with our dinner knife or emptying the water from abandoned air raid shelters. The latter task was back breaking and involved dropping an empty dustbin attached to a rope into the waterlogged shelter, heaving it up and carrying it to a drain. The weight was too much for sustained working and I soon drifted away from the senseless activity and kept my head down picking daisies. I relied upon the fact that we all looked alike in blue serge. Neither my fellow recruits, nor the NCO in charge, had been together long enough to recognise each other so my desertion from the allocated task managed to go undetected.

Finally, on 14 September a posting to Grading School, two and a half weeks after joining up, was announced and we could set our backs to Lancashire and travel cross-country to Lincolnshire. Again I have neither record or recollection of how.

Chapter Six

Grading School

The Grading School at RAF Digby was an outstation to RAF College, Cranwell, about 5 miles away, and the home of their engineer cadets. This south west corner of Lincolnshire is more gentle undulating and green then the harsher flatness of the Parts of Lindsey to the north - as we were to find out. After the dismal hutted accommodation of our previous station we enjoyed the comfort of a permanent brick built airfield. During our stay all cadets whether graded as pilots or navigators were to be given 12 hours of flying under instruction on Tiger Moths to assess their actual flying ability. We were given a single sheet of a log book on which to record our hours under instruction. Our stay at Digby lasted for 5 weeks and we were given flying tests at five and a half, eight and a half and eleven and a half hours of dual instruction. In the course of flying we had to be instructed in, and certified as competent to hand swing the propeller and my certificate dated 20 September is stuck in the log book. We also spent some time on the ground being given basic instruction on the various arts and mysteries of the flying profession and the machines we flew but much of the time we were at leisure sitting out in the sun waiting our turn. This was real flying, as it would have been like in WWI: an open cockpit with the wind rushing by, the more primitive instrument panel. Communication in flight was by hand signal or voice tube, it required hand swinging of the prop to start the engine and the petrol tank was overhead in the top wing with a stick float gauge. To fly we had the temporary issue of flying kit including the cumbersome Didcot heavy flying suit. I can be seen wearing it in the photo alongside the Tiger Moth. To my absolute delight my achievement was sufficient to be regraded as Cadet Pilot, although I did not manage to go solo as did one guy, but he had come from a university air squadron and had flown previously.

Memories of my stay here are dim. The classic photo of me with my foot on the overcome Tiger monster was taken by one of the civilian instructors - they were all civilian. With his eye on the main chance, this chap had a good little sideline taking our photo in beach photographer style, with a ready sale - this might be the only time we could pose as intrepid aviators before being thrown out from flying! I seem to remember that we lost one or two days to bad weather and I remember writing some, I thought, good prose about the depressing weather and silent aircraft slowly dripping oil on the hanger floor, to an old girl friend at SEEBoard. She didn't reply and later told me that her boyfriend said they were from a madman and tore the verses up. Some people have no soul and the art world and posterity is the loser. I wished I had kept them or copies. My recollection of Digby is of a rosy time between the periods of absolute austerity and hard discipline, one left behind at Padgate and with worse, yet unrealised, to come. I cannot remember if anyone was taken off flying as a result of this practical testing of ability but I think one or two originally graded as pilots were swopped over in the opposite direction to me.

We left on 23 October 1951 on posting to No. 2 Initial Training School at Kirton in Lindsey having notched up another stage in the process.

On a nostalgia trip in May 2007 I was able to revisit RAF Digby but nothing about the site was remembered. We did learn that this is the oldest, being the first, of the RAF airfields.

Chapter Seven

No 2 Initial Training School

We were back to being housed in wooden huts with winter approaching. The camp was stuck right out in the freezing cold countryside of North Lincolnshire. We were C flight, 2 Squadron, 2 Wing, 24 airmen to a hut plus the hut corporal who would also be our drill instructor. As the winter progressed our wet boots froze to the floor at night. Those cadets with beds opposite the pipe stoves were troubled by having everyone sitting on them to keep close to the stove to be warm. The fires glowed cherry red as the coke was shovelled in but slowly went out as they became unattended in the night. Obviously we had no inhibitions about lighting the stoves. Bull night here was a nightmare, and the discipline probably the harsher because as potential officers under training we had to know how to take it.

One of the rotten jobs was cleaning the ablution block. Not that it was unpleasant to clean because at all times it looked as if had just been cleaned! It was just the bull night routine that everything was scrubbed till it shone and no one could use the facilities until the inspection the following morning - difficult if taken short. Not only had the tiled floor to be scrubbed but it then had to be polished and then only way to get it dry in time was to use our own towels! I rebelled against such stupid authority and devised a cunning scheme. Inside the hut we were subject to the senseless shuffling along on the felt pads to preserve the high gloss on the flooring as previously described. So, as soon as the hut corporal was satisfied that we passed muster for the inspection the following day and went off with his drinking pals, I would join up my team of rebel supporters.

We became known as C Flight Square Dancing Team and I conceived the idea that if we could do something on this holy glazed floor to hit back at the ridiculous ritual then sanity and individual freedom might be restored. I had no idea of square dancing but knew that two lines faced each other and cavorted so it was not too difficult to devise a pattern to follow. So we did it on every bull night to the mortification of the other 16 hut members who thought the direst consequences would be brought down on us because of the damage to the shiny floor, but it never happened. Needless to say we did not dance shuffling on felt pads but with our boots on!

There were a few other kindred spirits with the will to break free of the prison camp mentality and it resulted in one memorable occasion. Our movements in camp were ruled by the Tannoy loudspeaker system. To signify the end of an announcement the speaker would say "Tannoy off": The words still ring in my ears. The loudspeaker system got us up at 6am with a reveille call and it was delivered in a very special and standardised way. One morning the reveille call came through at what seemed a ridiculously early time - and it was! The difference was that while the format was perfect the voice was plumy and unmistakably one of our course members who had somehow got into the radio station and made the broadcast at 2.15am instead of 6am getting the whole camp out of bed. He was a surprising chap who always looked a mess in his uniform, could not put his beret on properly or with the badge over the eye but was public school. There was hell to pay as a result as the radio station was in a top security part of the station. As in a prison of war camp this act of defiance kept us in high spirits for some time.

We were given to pranks on each other. Donald Wadkin was a real country boy from Leicestershire whose job had been making Stilton cheese. He was prone to going to bed early and some of the nasties spent a lot of time at his slumbering bedside pouring water into a mug close to his ear in the hope of promoting bed wetting - never successfully.

We were not given much leave during the whole of our stay at this camp and on the first occasion after 6 weeks we were given a weekend pass. The London boys organised coaches but I decided to take the train all the way but then on the Friday evening, right at the last minute all leave was cancelled and we had to report for jabs on Saturday instead - just another way of trying to break morale? Life was not all being physically strained to the limit on the parade ground and assault course. We had cross country running and route marches as well as bayonet drill! The last named was particularly nasty as it involved sticking the straw man through the middle and hitting his chin up with the rifle butt to make sure of finishing him off. But a more than equal amount of time was spent in the classroom on a full syllabus of study and instruction in airmanship, theory of flight, navigation, engineering, meteorology, officers' duties, man management, survival and firing live ammo on the rifle range. One instructor remains in the memory, a Flight Sgt who took us for engineering. After every point he made he would launch out on a fresh topic with the phrase, "Right you are, then - 'ere we 'ave", and he concluded the course with a memorable model solution to one of the final exam questions in the post-mortem that followed. Most of the students had been stumped by the question, "What is the purpose of the condenser in the aero engine?" His solution has stuck in my memory - "To prevent arcing and sparking across the contact breaker points". I had got it more or less right but not in his succinct wording.

As officer cadets, we not only practised shooting on the rifle range with the standard 303 rifles but also had a go at pistols, as when commissioned these side arms would be our standard weapon. It was very difficult to hit anything at the range with the pistols and we were all amazed when a hit, which we could see through the telescope, was recorded by one of our number. We were even more amazed when shooting was over and we went to recover our targets when the large black blowfly that had settled on our crack shot's target flew away and his was blank too!

When we eventually did get a mid-course

weekend leave I went home by train but disaster nearly struck on the way back. I had to change trains at Sleaford, quite late in the dark on Sunday night, and having been told which platform to board, I did so to find that five minutes after departure time we were still in the station. It transpired that only the front part of the train was going anywhere and had gone! The railway staff were very helpful in devising an alternative cross country route for me by which I narrowly averted overstaying my leave by scraping in before midnight when the pass expired. I think it entailed a lot of running on the final leg from the station. Penalty of overstaying leave is Jankers (with the probability of being thrown off the course and into the ranks).

As 11 November approached we prepared for a full parade on Remembrance Day at Lincoln Cathedral. Quite a buffing and polishing time as we paraded in white webbing, shiny buttons and gleaming boots. A word on the cult of boot polishing in the services may be timely. We were given two pairs of boots on entry, one of army-pattern and the other air force pattern, the latter being like carpet slippers compared to the former and easily brought to a shine because of the smooth leather. However, the army pattern were the ones for parades and worn daily but the problem was to get a high gloss on the dull and heavily grained leather surface. From new it required many hours and several tins of polish (not supplied) alternatively layering the polish on and melting it with a match and them spitting on the result and polishing with a circular motion of a duster covered finger. After weeks a reasonable standard could be achieved and individual methods varied considerably.

Our corporal DI's boots were incredible on parade but he had two pairs and kept his parade boots quite separate from his working boots. Sadly we were not so well provided for which meant that after route marching or assault course our highly polished boots were no more and we had to start again! There was also a fetish about shiny cap badges because until they had been polished very many times to wear off the fine edges of the brass casting they did not gleam. Lucky ones had badges given to them by dads who had previously served and had something to hand down but otherwise a ready solution such as emery paper was not obtainable while incarcerated in camp and ingenuity found other ways!

An old record card of physical fitness survives and a test dated 25 Oct shows that I wasn't very! I was still very thin from the long illness caused by the vaccination reaction following the Brighton smallpox outbreak at Christmas 1950 so maybe I was still not 100%. We had a lot of PT and out of the gym the football matches were well remembered for their spartan style. We would be out on the pitch very early in the morning with both goals only just discernible in the freezing mist which often blew up from the North Sea. Having been sorted into 2 teams of 11 we played vests v skins with the latter on losing the toss for the kick-off having to strip to the waist. There were no football shirts.

As Christmas approached we came to passing

out - I did so but a bit too near the borderline for comfort and only about 50% of us got through. Passing-out meant that I was now promoted to the rank of Acting Pilot Officer which was Gazetted 17 January, 1952 (the term means that all officer appointments are listed in the London Gazette which becomes the bible for all promotions and appointments) The half that failed had the unfortunate prospect of reverting for the rest of their service to the rank of ordinary aircraftman (A/C2) and being allocated a trade. Although we the successful ones were not yet out of the wood. If at any time we failed during our flying courses or did not qualify for wings then we too would be stripped of our acting rank and suffer the same fate which would be even more of a blow having enjoyed some of the delights of privilege.

Among my souvenirs around the time of the course ending are an autographed menu of the Christmas 1951 station lunch and the front cover of the official RAF Christmas card sent from Kirton-in-Lindsey. On the former the first signature is of David Nodder who, tragically died in a flying accident as later described.

We were given Christmas leave: I have no note of the duration and when we came back the end of course festivities were taking place. Another souvenir is a menu autographed by all our ground instructors at an end-of-course dinner we threw for them at the Berkeley Hotel, Scunthorpe on 5 January. As part of the evening's festivities, and at the specific request of our instructors, as our activity had become legend, we rolled back the carpet to perform our square dance for the last time. It must have been a thunderous performance because the hotel staff appeared to find out what was shaking the floor! 4 days later on 9 January 1952 I finally left the camp on 5 days' leave prior to posting to the next stage of the training.

On being granted our acting commissions we were issued with the National Service Pilot Officers' kit. - not the regulars' kit. We were expected to wear only battledress and were given a new one as best to augment those we already had and serve in place of the officer's No. 1 uniform. All other items relating to airman's uniform were handed in including my shiny army pattern boots - I kept the airforce pattern, (I think on payment). In addition we were issued with a Warrant Officer's greatcoat, an officer's raincoat and given a £2 glove allowance. An undated paper survives listing the kit issue to NS officers granted probationary commissions. When the military tailors arrived in the last days I splashed out on my No1 peaked cap - £4 from Allkit. Strictly speaking it was not official uniform to wear with battledress but it boosted ego.

When home on leave I visited my old colleagues in Hove and when Leslie Goodman heard that I was commissioned but would not be given a No1 uniform, he offered to lend me his as we were of the same build. I rushed it off to the tailors to have his Wing Commander's rings changed to my humble Pilot Officer's thin ring and his DFC and ribbons removed! Throughout my service I was very grateful to him for this. When in later months, we moved away from National Service only stations many of the NS officers were ostracised for having only a battledress to wear in the mess and on some occasions were excluded from the more formal functions.

All successful cadets were now split into three groups for flying training at 3 different flying schools and I was allocated to Booker, near High Wycombe.

Chapter Eight

Basic Flying Training School

I reported at RAF Booker on 15 January 1952 to this rather easy going camp - at least by comparison to the one just left. It was a typical camp built in wartime and the block built single storey huts were cold in winter but we had our own rooms. I travelled by train to High Wycombe station but I think we were not collected to report for duty but were told by the adjutant, on ringing in, to use the local bus. For the first time we were enjoying the less restricted lifestyle of officers and the comforts of the Officers' Mess. Our flying training was to be done by civilian instructors under an Airworks contract. The camp was run by a small establishment of RAF personnel and I think the CO was of Squadron Leader rank. Square bashing continued, albeit we were now addressed as "gentlemen" when given orders by the drill instructor, a portly Sergeant Jaques.

PE continued as part of the course work and the record card indicates that a retest for physical fitness showed that I had moved up a category to "good". It snowed a lot this winter so we had ground instruction when we could not fly. It was also the time when King George VI died. We had a full station funeral parade and Jaques let off a mortar as our gun salute. Photos show the snow and our flag at half mast. We also wore black arm bands for the duration of the mourning period.

We spent time between flights relaxing in the crew room which was warmed by the eponymous pipe stove and when our shoes got a bit wet in the snow and rain it was common to rest the feet on the stove. One or two dozed off in the heat and awoke to find the leather sole burnt through to the upper - it seems that wet leather and heat are not compatible.

One of the social graces of holding a commission was the leaving of cards on a plate at the door of the Officers' Mess when joining a new station or visiting one. It was a dying point of etiquette but we joined in and as Tony Sumner's dad was a printer he did cards for us. They were in beautiful engraved copper plate, I still have the plate and spare cards, and, as with the custom of junior officers we are shown on them as Mr.

It was ten days before all the formalities and the necessary ground instruction were completed before the flying programme started. I went solo after 5 hours of dual instruction. It was a great feeling when, after the second dual flight of the day practising circuits and bumps, Mr Lock my instructor climbed out, fastened his loose straps up tight and told me to take it off for a circuit and landing.

One skill we were taught was flying on instruments only. We would have eventually to take a White Card instrument rating test without which we could not qualify as pilots. Cloud conditions were simulated by erecting yellow panels in the aircraft round the pupil's sight line and him donning coloured goggles the colour combination of which totally blocked the view outside of the cockpit. Instrument flying would be done on both full instrument panel or limited panel, made possible by turning the aircraft over and toppling the giros of all the instruments leaving only the basic ones:- compass, turn & slip indicator and airspeed indicator which were not giro activated, still operating. These were the basic instruments with which the Tiger Moth had been equipped. Eventually the giros in the toppled instruments would start to operate again but it took about ten or fifteen minutes for them to do so. I became very good at flying on instruments, particularly as I did not fall prey to the "turns", which was the more likely to happen without full instrumentation. This is a peculiar sensation and comes about when, imperceptibly to your ear balance mechanism, one wing is allowed to drop, the process being so gradual that you are not aware of it happening. Reading the error on your instruments you then suddenly correct the controls to fly straight and level but the balance in the ear reacts to the sudden correction by now telling you that you are in a turn the other way. You must believe your instruments or get into real trouble.

On the social side, it was early on in my Booker flying days that I acquired the nickname of "Hank". We had among us one very nasty course member who specialised in putting everyone down. In the afternoon, if there was time between flying, we would return to the Mess for tea and invariably the T/V would be on - only one channel in those black and white days.

Being tea time it was also children's hour and a popular animated serial of the day, about Mexican Pete the Bad Bandit who was up to no good until Cowboy Hank rode by to put things right, was often showing. Hank was a bit odd looking so our nasty one sneered that I looked just like him. To the nasty one's annoyance my friends adopted it as a term of endearment and so it stuck for most of my flying days.

During the winter I went down with 'flu and was confined to the sick bay for 2 or three days. In the bed alongside was a course member and fellow sufferer and on one of the days he asked if I would mind him turning on the radio to listen to "Women's Hour" as his mother was to appear on it that afternoon. Imagine his horror - he curled up and hid under the bedclothes - when his mother spoke of her son who had just been commissioned but had to wear a silly battledress because no proper officer's uniform was being issued apart from £2 given to him to buy a pair of gloves. This earth-shattering interview apparently did nothing to get their Lordships to change their mind and we remained officially clothed in battledress for our two years. Connected to this comment about our second class uniform issue is the renegade unofficial photo session for which I again was responsible. Early on in the course we were told by our Chief Ground Instructor (CGI) to assemble for an official course photograph. We all thought it would be a splendid chance to show off our new peaked caps and everyone to turn up wearing one. Our CGI only did things by the book and, as I mentioned earlier, he considered us to be improperly dressed so were sent away to come back wearing berets. However, I did have the last word and got everyone to come back wearing their peaked caps and the photograph was taken with my faithful box camera and we ignored the official version when available to buy copies.

When up solo and looking for a bit of fun with any colleagues who were also not flying dual with their master we used to rendezvous over the cement factory at Aylesbury. It was an easily found landmark because of the smoke streaming from its chimney and to let others know we were there a brief snatch of "On Top of Old Smokie" was sung over the R/T. If it was Taffy Phillips who met you things could get a bit hairy because he would fly straight at you and his demonic laugh would come over the R/T as he broke away at the last minute. One area we were prohibited from flying over was Diana Dors' nearby house on the River Thames as she was often on a sun lounger round her swimming pool.

The log of our flying hours was kept by a couple of young ladies sitting in their timekeepers' hut situated at the edge of the field close to the usual direction of take-off being the prevailing wind direction on this grass field. Lots of joking took place round the hut while waiting to fly and I have a picture of Olive, one of the young timekeepers, taking the horseplay in good part. Her colleague was a stunner but sadly no photo!

We commenced night flying instruction in the last weeks of the course on two separate nights which was another milestone in our training. It was quite jolly and had a wartime feel about it because the runway was marked out on the grass by gooseneck flares - like large oilcans with a spout and a wick that burned with a yellow flame. To guide you on final approach two sets of portable coloured lights were set up at the start of the runway and if they were showing 2 greens then you were on the right glide path, other colours or only one green plus a colour meant you were wrong. After 2 goes with the instructor I had 45 minutes of circuits and bumps on my own and on the second night went solo again.

Mr Lock was my instructor up until the halfway test and then I became Mr Hill's pupil. He was a great pilot and could do all sorts of clever things. Older than others he had flown every type of aircraft and told me that at one time he had the job of flying repaired crashed aircraft to see if they were fit to re-enter wartime service. On one occasion we took off in a very strong wind - I think he was a master green and could fly in any weather he chose. No one else was up so we took off and our combined speed and the head wind speed enabled him to go backwards along the runway almost on the point of stall until the start when he landed again! Another time he demonstrated the falling leaf descent where you fall out of the sky by stalling into an incipient spin from side to side - a most violent manoeuvre. We got on very well and I think his intervention helped me stay on the course after the final test foul-up.

I think it was on 8th April that I was booked to take my final flying test and although I was reasonably confident of passing out the day ended in disaster with the very real prospect of being sent home! It so happened that the day started very foggy and we all sat in the crew room waiting for it to clear, not the most happy of circumstances when expecting to take a test. By lunchtime things had not improved so we were sent off to the Mess for lunch. After the meal I was returning to the crewroom and when almost there I was met by a fellow student coming back from the crew room who told me that flying was scrubbed for the day. It was not an infrequent happening during flying training because it was usually reckoned that if the sun had not burned off the clagg by 1 or 2pm it was not going to. So I returned to my room, changed, caught the bus to High Wycombe and went to the cinema. Imagine my horror when I came out into bright sunshine and a clear blue sky! I got back to camp quickly and reported to the flight office to present my apologies and explain my reason for failing to appear and a very stern Mr Howard, the Chief Flying Instructor (CFI) told me he would deal with me in the morning. Fortunately, on the next day I was exonerated. My fellow student came forward to confirm the story and I was flying again on a lengthy revision and practice with Mr Hill. This was followed by a cross country solo and on the third and last flight of the day I was allowed to take the final test with Howard, the CFI - the rest, as they say, is history!

My final flight from Booker on 10th April (and

incidentally my last in a Chipmunk for a long time) was memorable and I was involved as the most senior student available. I think, because of the delay in my final test and the few days I lost to flu the others had already gone. It was coming up to the Easter holiday and one of the instructors, Mr Paine, was trying to wangle a free lift to his home town of Cardiff. The powers-that-be decided that they could authorise a flight to Cardiff on the basis of the dual instruction carried out on the way down and a student's solo cross country back. And so we took off and landed safely and Paine attended to the formalities and refuelling at Cardiff. Then, goodbyes were said and I was off on my own. It was a civilian airfield and had a hard runway, something that I had to use for the first time - I should explain that on a grass field it matters not if you waver or wander a little on take-off. Here I had noticed that there was a distinct step between the runway edge and adjoining grass so I had to keep straight despite a bad cross-wind. Of course cross-winds are never a problem on grass because the take off is in the wind direction while, although fixed runways point into the prevailing wind direction the winds do not always oblige! - I was learning more about my trade. Eventually I was given clearance and opened up the tap and countering the prop torque and wind direction to keep straight, I lifted off more or less straight with the bogie of going over the edge behind me. It was then that I saw looming ahead the tall cooling towers of Cardiff power station. A climbing turn brought me safely round 180° and on track for home which I obviously made without getting lost because the flight time was 5 minutes less than the outward journey.

I went home for the Easter weekend, or a short spot of leave, that evening because the return half of a rail ticket issued on 10 April survives amongst the memorabilia. It seems from the detail on the ticket that either we had a free warrant or we got a reduced rate for rail travel. I think this was my last day at Booker, although the Record of Service shows me on strength until 21 April, and I cleared all my effects to take home with me expecting the new posting to be effective directly after Easter.

The old papers record that Holme-on-Spalding-Moor was not ready for us so I must have had leave extended by a week after the bank holiday. I do not remember going back to Booker, which would already be involved with a new intake, and it was usual to be sent home on leave whilst postings were sorted out. In this case our new station was being taken out of mothballs and was not quite ready.

I heard that all the two thirds of the students on our course at Kirton Lindsey who had qualified for basic flying training at Anstey and Syerston had been scrubbed in the course of training and were back in the ranks. By the grace of God another stage had been successfully negotiated and I now had 72 hours of flying under my belt, 43 of which were solo and nearly four at night. Not only that but I had moved up the league table in the end of course combined ratings for flying and ground tests.

Chapter Nine

Flying Training School

On 22 April 1952 I set off from Brighton station yet again, this time to York Station and on to Flying Training School at Holme-on-Spalding-Moor. It had just been reopened and we were the first course to pass through. It was a typical wartime camp with buildings of a prefabricated nature but a proper airfield with runways. During the war many of the famous bomber squadrons and their aces had flown from here. We shared accommodation and I think there were four of us to a room. We were to fly Airspeed Oxfords to get our wings and the current thinking was that by doing our advanced training on twin piston-engined aircraft we would the better fly twin-engined jets at the jet conversion stage. Some muddled thinking, if the theory were true, because while we could learn the delights of asymmetric flight in the Oxford, it was not an aircraft which could do aerobatics. On the contrary, Oxfords had a very bad spin recovery record so that we could never practise the manoeuvres which would be second nature to fighter pilots. Other Flying Training Schools were equipped with Harvards which, in essence, were long obsolete semi-fighter aircraft extensively used as a trainer and fully manoeuvrable. Having said that, the Oxford was lovely to fly and I would have been quite happy to have progressed to transport aircraft as a prelude to getting into commercial aviation. But it was not to be and the fighter route was the one chosen for me.

It took 6 1/2 hours instruction before my first solo on the Oxford on 1st May. I do not remember anyone doing it in much less time and before we could go we had to be certified as competent on the systems, fire and abandoning procedures and to carry out a blind cockpit drill.

On my first flight with F/O Jack Burry I was given a 5 minute taster of flying in cloud. In my log book can be seen that I had the pleasure of an hour's solo flight on my 19th birthday. Up to this time Jack Burry had been my instructor but he was posted about May and I flew mostly solo with some instruction from five of the other instructors until mid July when P/O Bevis took over who was not very experienced. On 10th July we had our first flight together in the day and night flying started that evening. On our first night flight together Bevis nearly caused a fatal accident. At night taxiing aircraft were marshalled with the aid of ground crew using illuminated blue wands. We were awaiting our turn to move off when another aircraft was being manoeuvred forward and Bevis thought it was we who were being called forward with the result that the ground crewman acting as marshal came close to having his head chopped off by our propellers! I managed to shout to him to brake in time.

After 3 1/2 hours of night dual flying I was off on my own - great fun. In total I flew over 13 hours at night and half of it solo which included a 3-point cross country of nearly 2 hours and another of 1 hour 40 minutes with a call to make a diversionary landing at an unknown airfield in mid flight. During the first of these tragedy struck. That evening David Nodder was feeling very tired and went to sleep on his bed before we were called down to the crew room. After he took off we did not see him again and at daybreak his aircraft was discovered spread across a couple of fields and it was thought that he fell asleep at the controls.

On 4 or 5 flights I was under dual instruction with Flt/Sgt Smith and as recorded later I had an unexpected meeting with him after leaving RAF when flying on a commercial flight to Jersey.

The following notes record some of my recollections from flying days at Holme-on-Spalding-Moor:-

28 August was a momentous day, not just because it was my anniversary of joining up, but because on my flight with Flt Lt Colahan of the Central Flying School (CFS). It could have been my last! The object of students flying with one of these gods from the CFS high altar of flying was to check out that our instructors were doing a proper job. I have to explain that the rudder pedals on the Oxford were adjustable back and forward and wound in or out by using a foot on a wheel at each side of the rudder bar. Unfortunately, "Lofty" Howard (another coincidence about him is mentioned at the end), well over 6ft tall, had flown the previous sortie. It was "up and away quickly" with this big cheese from CFS, and when it was my turn Howard climbed out, I climbed in and took the seat with

engines still running. Obviously Howard had wound the pedals right forward and I had no time to wind the pedals back. In the course of the flying I had to demonstrate a stall and recovery from the incipient spin that followed. I had full rudder on but she was still going over even though my leg was fully stretched and I was pushing with my toes. In a rather ill temper, Colahan shouted at me for not applying full rudder and slammed the rudder bar over with such full force that the rudder cables snapped! We were in a serious position about to go into a full spin with no rudder, without which control it would have been impossible to recover and baling out would have been the only option. However, Colahan managed to recover by applying full asymmetric power with nose hard down and we came back to base for an emergency landing. He looked terribly green all the way back and refused my offer to fly it part of the way. All hell broke loose with the Engineering Officer after we landed because a defect like this just should not have happened despite the intemperate action of the pilot. But this was a very old plane built in 1932 and I cannot recall any disciplinary action resulting from the complaint.

Asymmetric flight was mentioned earlier and involved extensive use of the rudder. Hard rudder was necessary to counter the loss of an engine and we practised it by throttling right back on one.

A nasty fatal accident that nearly got me too happened whilst waiting to take-off with my instructor one day. We were in a holding position right by the runway when 2 aircraft came in on top of one another. The aircraft collided on finals and the one underneath had its tail chopped off. It fell about 100yrds from our stationary position and just seconds later it would have happened overhead. I have no record apart from an undated press cutting and photos of wreckage. The pilot from a junior course to ours was killed instantly. It was an incredible sight as the mortally wounded aircraft first rose up vertically then plunged nose down into the ground.

Anther fatality during the course was Jackson, not someone I got on with. He was supposed to be an adventurous pilot but got out of control and baled out too low so that his parachute could not open. His parents had just bought him a red Singer sports car and it was some time after his death before the vehicle was taken away from outside the mess - until it was it remained a sombre reminder of his accident from being reckless.

Mayes was another course member who came to grief but fortunately without injury. What he was trying to do I know not but on the final approach with wheels down he touched down in a rough field about a mile from the start of the runway and promptly flip over upside down.

Flg Off Fern was not my regular instructor but I flew under his instruction on 5 occasions in the early days. He was in the habit of taking his regular student pilots out to the start of the runway to watch and learn from the competence or otherwise of how other trainee pilots were landing. I was solo on circuit and bumps one day and, apparently, the excellence of my landings was remarked upon and the pupils told to find out who was flying the machine. Nothing official was ever said to me but my colleagues told me about it later and the fact that Fern had said to them that he was not surprised to hear it was me! - great confidence booster.

Apart from our flying one of the requirements of our training was time spent in the Link Trainer and between 3rd March and 16th September I did 16 1/2 hours in the little closed tin box which responded as an aircraft being flown on instruments. It was nothing like the modern sophisticated simulators. Occasionally one of the flying instructors would sneak into the room and put on a gale force wind which would cause havoc to your carefully judged flight path!

One of the diverting activities during the course was an escape and evasion exercise over a weekend with groups of 4 students led by their flying instructor. In our case it was P/O Bevis who had just returned from sick leave and not really with it. The rules were that we would be dropped off from the transport at regular intervals on Friday night around 6pm and about 20 miles from base and we had to make our way back by Sunday morning. The whole of the TA, army, police specials and any other officials that could be persuaded to take part were out to capture us. They were to occupy all key points and if caught we ended up in "prison camp" although there were supposed to be 3 safe houses for refuge. Their side was not supposed to take up position until 7pm giving us at least 30 minutes to get off the road and start our trek across fields. This part of Yorkshire is very flat round the Humber estuary and full of dykes and Bevis led us through some of them by which time we were wet up to the waist without getting very far. We came to a light bridge and after debate Bevis went across because it should not yet have been manned but it was and they nabbed him. He had the presence of mind to let out a loud hullabaloo to warn us so we retired into the shadows but not before an attempt at retribution. The enemy's Ford 8 was parked close to the bridge so I lifted the bonnet and removed the rotor of the distributor and put it on the cylinder block to make their journey to a warm place a little delayed. If the enemy were now in position I decided that we had little chance of getting all the way and it would be better just to concentrate on escaping capture. The others fell in with the plan and we march in the dark, not really sure of direction because the map, compass and torch had been lost with Bevis. At first light I came to an old quarry with a wooden hut. We got in and found the old familiar pipe stove inside. So with a hunt through pockets for scraps of paper and the fruits of a fuel scouting party out looking for anything to burn we soon had a blaze going to dry out and warm while eating some of our iron rations. We rested for early part of the morning and set out again using minor roads and finger posts to guide us making much better progress because we were nearer to the starting point than the end and much of the heat had been taken off to concentrate nearer home. It was obvious at first light that we could not get back by the deadline so I flagged someone down for a lift nearer to camp and phoned in to be collected. We ended up among the few at liberty because the enemy had jumped the gun. Even the safe houses were all captured but that was because some idiots revealed the details of their whereabouts under interrogation. Unfortunately, our achievement was lessened when one of our group blabbered about how we had done it. My view was that evading was the key thing and timescale of less importance and we had done a good job when the others were being rounded up in their scores early on.

At some time Mike Neal brought his old 1928 Morris Minor to camp and at weekends four of us had outings in it to Hornsey and other parts of the Yorkshire coast as the photographs reveal.

I often joined in on manic visits to the local pubs in someone's 1928 Austin 7. Between 7 and 9 people could be got in but it involved someone doing the gear change with someone else on the pedals. Often as we shot into the main road accusations would break out as to whose foot was supposed to be on the brake pedal! On one occasion after one such carousal the double doors were opened up late at night/early morning and the car driven into the Officers' Mess where it was found on the following morning with the usual hell-to-pay results - I was not involved on that occasion.

On the base we had an accounting officer who

was always happy in the mess and a leading light during dining-in night. One of the entertainments was a singing game. Limericks were sung followed by a chorus ending with "Sing us another one, Just like the other one, Sing us another one, Do---You" at which point the soloist would point to another member and if you could not think of one it cost a round and something more embarassing! Never lost for a rhyme, he lived with his wife in a caravan in the grounds of the local pub and at some time our Flight Commander asked us to boycott the pub in future as the publican had evicted him apparently without reason. Some time later the reason became obvious when our Accounting Officer was arrested and jailed for embezzlement, probably trying to keep up with his blowsy blonde wife.

York was the nearest town for recreation, shopping and entertainment including a few concerts. I cannot remember if we travelled by taxi, somebody's car, bus or train. Betty's bar was a great favourite with its all-round mirrored walls signed by hundreds of aircrew including so many who never came back from wartime ops. We always had tea in the Willow Tea Rooms. Both sadly are no more but I believe that the mirrors are ensconced in a museum somewhere.

After a total of 203 hours of flying my Flying Badge was awarded on 24th September 1952 along with my White Card instrument rating, just under 13 months since joining up.

My last flight from the station on the 18

September was in a dual Meteor. We had been told what Commands we would be allocated to and the fighter boys were given a 45 minute taster of what was in store at the next stage in an aircraft especially flown in for us. It was quite an exciting thing to fly in a jet for the first time.

Graduation day was 24th September when wings were awarded to me. Of the 51 who started the course 5 did not make it to wings and 2 had died. I had moved up to 10th in the passing out rankings. Dad, Mum & girlfriend Sheila drove up to witness the graduation and after tea in the mess we were free to go home and on leave until recalled. We drove home through the night in the Ford 8, Dad and I taking turns at the wheel and we picked up 2 punctures on the way!

Successful completion of the course meant being Gazetted in the substantive rank of Pilot Officer - and being given an additional glove allowance of £1!
So ended one of the happiest times. It was a friendly station and we were led by a fine body of instructors - between them our instructors and senior officers had 10 DFCs. So much of the enjoyment of this posting was the sheer delight of flying the Oxford which I had learned to handle really well.

Chapter Ten

Advanced Flying School

My new posting came through and once again I commenced the journey from Brighton station this time to Doncaster. From the town we drove the short distance past Doncaster race course. I reported for duty on 7th October 1952 at No 215 Advanced Flying Training School, RAF Finningley.

Here we would undertake our jet conversion, the theory being, as already explained, that having done our training on twin engined aircraft we could more readily adapt to the Meteor. As I have said, in my view this was a flawed theory because the old Oxford was not an aerobatic plane and suited to more sedate flying whereas the Harvard would have got us into a fighter frame of mind.
We were now in a permanent brick built airfield and much more comfortable than when stationed on the previous sites. Geoff Rothon and I shared a room and a batman.

My first instructor was Flt Lt Johnson and we did not hit it off from the start- an unpleasant sneering man and I came close to being scrubbed. My log book records my last 2 flights with Johnson were on 31 October and that I made the last sortie of that day with Flg Off Rawlinson who presumably had been detailed to check out if I was as bad as Johnson made out. Obviously, I wasn't because having flown 5 1/2 hours of dual with my tormentor, Master Pilot Vose took me under his wing. (Master Pilot was a Warrant Officer rank created towards the end of the war and bestowed upon the best and experienced NCO pilots but without the complex admin duties of the Warrant Officer rank).

Vose was an amazing chap, tall and heavily built, hard drinking and womanising, no respect for authority but a brilliant pilot, master green and the most experienced. After 3 hours under his tutelage I went solo and I think did not look back.

Rawlinson was a strange chap, affable, one of us boys in the crew room but seemingly in the throes of a nervous breakdown on the ground . In the air he was strict, precise and demanding. He must have been one of the instrument flying experts because I had one session with him and another on SCT (I cannot remember what that stands for).

Among the recreational activities we were able to visit the test match against India at Headingly over a weekend. We found the female students at the university were the ice cream sellers so we had to keep buying so that they would sit and talk to us.

Eddie Smeeth, our Flight Commander, was a kind chap who gave us lifts to London in his Hillman saloon when we had weekend leave.

Finningley in winter was a bad place for flying because of the fog exacerbated by the terrible industrial smog of SouthYorkshire. We spent many days enjoying the "lovely clamp" - days of waiting for it to clear although when we did fly it got me into serious trouble on more than occasion. On one of the bad times in the smog, which constantly bedevilled us in flying from Finningley, I was practising stall turns. This manoeuvre requires a sight of the horizon and there was none. I got it all wrong fell out of it in a spin from which the Meteor is infamously bad to recover, said to be two turns and it won't come out. I did not know if I was in an inverted spin and the control column was thrashing around, another of its vices. Fortunately I had not put the jet flames out by sliding back on my tail and by some fluke using power corrected.

Another time I was returning to base and just could not see where I was in the murk with fuel down to below that permitted for joining the circuit. So I had to send out a Pan (second most serious emergency call) for "Pigeons to Finningley" (course to fly to base) and just got in.

A member of the course above us, Monro, did run out of fuel and severely damaged his aircraft in a crash landing. He told us that, completely out of control, he touched down heavily on some grass rose high again over the top of a removal van that was travelling along the adjacent main road and crashed on the other side. After extricating himself from the cockpit he found the van driver running up to embrace him for his skill in saving his life. Monroe commented that it was pure luck as he had no control over the aircraft!

It was the practice for one of the instructors to

do a weather check before flying could commence. On this occasion Flt Sgt Harvey decided to take two of us up with him on his check flight for a spot of formation flying. Due to the continual bad visibility the course was getting behind and I suppose he thought we could get a little more flying in and from the ground the conditions looked OK. However after about 30 minutes a thick fog bank rolled in from the east and so we returned to base. Over the runway we broke in traditional 20 second breaks, Harvey was in the clear but I went straight into the fog and visibility was very bad and the ground had disappeared. Standard procedure is to fly a timed circuit and turn 90° over some identifiable feature on the ground. I tried it but could not make out anything and so went round on timed legs and compass bearings. On finals I asked the runway control to send up yellow flares but could not spot them and then through the gloom saw a hanger looming up ahead and pulled up just in time! But I now knew where I was - about 800yrds off the runway - and did a very low level circuit with 90° turns, almost lined up but with a violent kick on the rudder at the end and was down with just enough fuel to get back to dispersal. Unbeknown to me, Pete Frame the other wingman, saw immediately what happened to me and did not break but stayed on my tail because my friends had great faith in my flying ability! He got in too but ran out of fuel on the runway. Needless to say, further flying was abandoned for the day and our flight leader kept a low profile.

I also ran foul of a new CO, Squadron Leader

Terry Ormiston, on one occasion. He was newly promoted and joined us just before Christmas. I had flown with him once before and on 22nd January , after a couple of solo flights - one in formation - I flew my intermediate handling test with him in the late afternoon. I think he wanted to make his mark - Bader fashion - for as soon as we had landed he stormed into the crew room, called us all together and proceeded to lambast me for a lack lustre performance. Maybe my old Oxford habits of too much straight and level aroused him but this was to be his pep talk to the flight! Afterwards Vose told me to forget it and said that when Ormiston was on a squadron he was said to have taken off one day and was clearly heard by Control giving instructions and urging his formation team to tighten up though no-one was with him! Probably too much sherbet at lunch!

One day Vose, who was a law unto himself, took me up on a day when there was a strong gale blowing and Eddie Smeeth, our flight commander had stopped flying for the day because the cross wind was too strong.. At Finningley we had 2 main runways, one of 2000yrds and the second about 1800yrds. A third, short one of 1400yrds made up the triangle but it was never used because it was just not long enough for the Meteor's safe take-off run or landing. The wind was about 45 knots down the short runway and without more ado, Vose taxied out and to the amazement of the tower called for take-off clearance on the short runway. We made it after a lot of holding on the brakes at full power and wind buffeting, as my continuing life on this planet is testimony, but we landed on the main runway and the crosswind had us on a 45° approach. I have done some heady flying with really competent instructors.

One day a curious thing happened when Vose and I went out to take over a Meteor from Eddie Smeeth and pupil. Smeeth casually announced that he had dropped a pair of scissors in the cockpit and could not find them. An incredulous Vose asked what he had been doing with scissors and the answer was trimming his fingernails! Up we went and at height Vose said he would turn upside-down to try and find them if I would catch them. The scissors settled on the cockpit roof too far behind my head to reach so we turned back over and the scissors fell right into the hole where my control column passed through the floor which meant that neither stick could be pulled back. I undid my straps to lean right forward to grab the scissor handles as Vose pushed the stick right forward in a steep dive so I could yank them free! It worked and Vose declined to return them to the Flight Commander and told me to keep them as a memento. I still have them and use them to cut my nails.

Another diversion came from the course above us. Just as their course was finishing they embarked upon a "rite of passage" and dangerous dare. Each of them had to take off and keeping low do a roll off the top back over the airfield. We all watched them in fascination and they all made it, some a bit wobbly off the top but management got wind of it and, as low level aerobatics, was strictly banned for future.

One of the pilots in the course above us was killed in a flying accident in midwinter. It was cold and snow lay on the ground when, it was thought, he came in on a very tight turn at too low a speed and just fell out of the sky onto his wing tip and cartwheeled. I cannot remember his name but we called him "creeping Jesus" because of the shoes he wore. Crepe-soled footwear had just come into fashion and reluctantly been adopted by the Air Ministry as acceptable optional uniform. He was a regular and so had plenty of kit allowance. I was involved, as orderly officer of the day, in travelling into Doncaster to attend to the death formalities. First I was in difficulty with the Registrar of Deaths because he had him listed as Ray and I could not confirm that that was his full christian name or short for Raymond. More trouble at the undertakers because he was to be embalmed and the coffin taken to his home town up North. They had difficulty because no one had told them that the corpse was headless! *"Oh! who would be an orderly upon an orderlies' day?",* (quote). Something that struck as bizarre at the time was his family's use of the Coop undertakers presumably to get their dividend. In maturity I think it an excellent idea! One problem with the crash recovery team was that they could not locate one of the engines. I expect also that one unfortunate farmer would have got a shock when the snows melted and a grinning head looked up at him from his cabbage patch!

Among the records accumulated from the

course are: a Meteor fuel range chart, various drills relating to the Meteor certified on 31 October 1952.and an anoxia demonstration carried out in a pressurised tank on 9th October. - these have been stuck in the log book. We also had sessions on management and problem solving and a Form 3948 survives.

A comment on the joys of asymmetric flight - full details of the procedures on losing an engine on multi-engined aircraft is given in Pilots Notes General. Often an instructor would suddenly close one throttle, when at a safe height to do so, on take-off or when coming in to land to simulate sudden engine failure. Just to do it for real they sometimes turned the flame right off and you did not have an idling engine on which to increase power so had to get it right. These more extreme tests are recorded in the log book and on one occasion to make it even more difficult I was flying on instruments at the time - but not trying to land!

I have a complete set of lecture notes issued to us and they must have been extensively used in swotting for the final exam. The weekend flyers of 601 County of Yorkshire auxiliary squadron were based in the crewroom next to ours and they also flew Meteors, but the latest. When the weekends were to o bad for flying their pilots sat in the crew room trying to break the record of the most bottles of champagne drunk in the day - I think it got beyond16.

The "D" Flight Christmas party is well recorded in photos. All the students: Taffy Phillips, Pete

Frame, Brian Collison, Me and Geoff Rothon are in one and the other has Flt Sgt Harvey, Eddie Smeeth, Flt Lt Liskutin and Doug Rawlinson, our flying instructors, prominent among us. Vose can be seen at the back playing the fool. All the other bods in the photos are our groundcrew who presented us with "Christmas presents". Mine was a crude model of an Avro delta fighter (which was currently being trialled to come into service as the next generation fighter aircraft) with the message "May you enjoy........................, as you fly your delta about the sky" (all I can remember) as the aluminium scraps and message are long lost. (The record of XI squadron, attached, shows that conversion to Delta aircraft did take place). The only other present I can recall was given to Geoff Rothon. He had great trouble with G-forces and, when strongly applied by his instructor, was known to black out. So he was given an old set of corsets to wear as an anti-G suit.

I completed the course after 70 hours of jet flying and satisfied Ormiston on my final test which was to be my last flight at Finningley on 4 February, 1953. That Final Test was an extraordinary affair because a massive weather front was coming up and I expected it to be postponed. I suppose that the CO was showing me that I would now be an operational fighter pilot who flew in all weathers. I took off into the blackest cumulonimbus cloud I had ever seen that went from about 1000ft to over 30000ft. The colours were beautiful. We spent the flight doing all the drills and aerobatics alternately in torrential rain and sudden bright periods. After

40 minutes we were down and I had thrown the aircraft all over the place on the way. I passed.

Earlier, on 30 January I had had my White Instrument Rating card renewed (and endorsed for jet aircraft). This was quite a long drawn out exercise involving a 1 hour check by the flight Commander and the test of 1hr 10 minutes to follow - both with a long range ventral tank. This was quite an exhausting day because it had started with a solo flight as part of a formation.
The training course officially ended on 9 February. Until 13 March we were transferred to Station strength although for much of the time we were sent on leave but not without yet another inoculation,. We were recalled to be told of our postings and six of us were to report to 2nd Tactical Air Force in Germany, an announcement that had us dancing round the table at the prospect of an overseas posting!

It was very unusual that we were not first going to Operational Conversion Units to be trained in aerial warfare. The Russians were causing great concern at this point of history and it seemed that, in WWI fashion, we were being sent to the front line to learn our trade in battle if necessary. In National Service terms we had already spent three quarters of our call-up period in training and no more time could be spared.

Chapter Eleven

Operational Flying and an Introduction to 2ⁿᵈ Allied Tactical Air Force

In some ways the story from now on is not quite as exciting as were the previous stages of aircrew training. It was a combination of things. It was not the best time to be joining the squadron as it was re-equipping with the very latest fighter aircraft the Venom, the first squadron to do so, and had the job of sorting out the operational problems. We had, initially, only 6 of the new aircraft for all the squadron pilots. The fact that I was NS and with little time left to demob did not endear me. Soon after I joined we had a change of command from Sqn/Ldr Seaton to Sqn/Ldr Batchelar. Finally, as a member of the General Duties Branch, as were all aircrew, we had admin duties to perform as well as flying, something we had largely been absolved from as students. Another thing which affected performance was the relatively short time that a jet fighter could stay in the air which meant that flying hours did not accumulate at a fast rate.

A shorter train journey sent me on my way from Brighton to Harwich. It was a very early start and to carry all my belongings I had bought a cheap trunk in a Gardner Street junk shop and all the flying kit was in an aircrew kitbag. I had to find a porter to help and someone from the parcels office did the honours. At Harwich we boarded the Empire Wansbeck, an old troop carrier, to sail overnight to the Hook of Holland

and as an officer I was allocated a cabin, shared with an army officer, for the night. All the decks were packed with other ranks making the best of an uncomfortable journey. It was my first experience of the Military Transport Organisation and they seemed pretty efficient. From The Hook we travelled by train through, I think, to Bremen where we changed to travel to Buckeburg. 2nd TAF HQ. On the platform we witnessed a sombre sight as a coffin was taken out of a train, placed on a gun carriage draped with an RAF flag. We heard that it was a pilot who went vertically into an autobahn and was now on his way home. The six of us were still travelling together and we were collected at the station in a very efficient Volkswagen personnel carrier; centre section had passenger seats and the rear a large hold to carry luggage etc. We were accommodated in the late evening in a massive and sombre ex Weirmacht barrack block and only had 2 nights to stay. I have no recollection of how or where I was fed since leaving Brighton. We reported at the HQ building the next morning and a tiresome place it proved to be. Hardly anyone held the rank below Squadron Leader and there was enough scrambled egg on hats to feed an army! We spent the day saluting but at least had our next posting - to 2 Group at RAF Sundern and after breakfast were on our way. Here we spent a week being briefed on all manner of things and we taken into the control room. Reminded of our secrecy obligation, it was then disclosed that the Russians had just shot down our Lincoln bomber in the Berlin air corridor and the situation was more than tense. Later, the same was done to an American aircraft on their southern sector border. We had a session with the Wing Commander who was in charge of air accident statistics. There was increasing concern over the increasing frequency and similarity of these incidents, not all ending in fatalities. The answer, it was thought, would be to publish details of every accident for every pilot in the Group to read. He wanted 2 volunteers from among us to stay at 2 Group and analyse the type of accident and promulgate it to squadrons to stop it happening. Fortunately one of our number had been in insurance and was nominated and his friend stayed with him so only 4 of us remained for the final posting to a squadron.

Chapter Twelve

11 Squadron

Phillips and Collison had been allocated to 5 Squadron flying Vampires. I reported to 11 Squadron, also at RAF Wunstorf, on 24 March with P/O Carter, somebody I had not come across before and I cannot remember his antecedents. This was a master airfield and lovely permanent site with very comfortable quarters where I had the services of a batwoman provided by the locally recruited German Civilian Organisation. During WWII Wunstorf had been one of the major bases of the Luftwaffe and, as witnessed by the miles of concrete hardstanding, had subsequently played a major part in the Berlin airlift. At the squadron office we found that most of the pilots were not there but in Spain or other continental countries as part of a top aerobatic team attending air displays and showing off their new toys. One thing I did find out, and of morbid interest, was what happened to the pilot I was replacing. The good news was that he had not been swept up in little pieces but was a Sgt pilot serving time in Colchester for being caught selling tyres from the transport section to the Germans! I joined No. 11 as they were being equipped with the new Venom in place of Vampires - the first squadron to do so. Only 8 aircraft had been built by de Havilland at that time. The squadron had been allocated 6 and 2 were being kept for extensive trials at the factory. It was 2 weeks before I got into the air. After the return the CO and his top pilots were flying the Venoms on acceptance trials so I had to make do with one of the old Vampires. Before letting me loose they checked me out in the T11 dual version Vampire and I had a couple of sorties on instruments in the dual Meteor also on squadron strength. On those early dual flights aerial combat was demonstrated so I began to learn the art of warfare. Once, when up in the Meteor we were asked over the R/T to go and investigate an unidentified aircraft. The captain - I was flying as second pilot - immediately regretted that we could not do so as we were low on fuel. I pointed out to him that we had plenty plus the long range tank and learned my first lesson in a combat zone - he had excused us because we were unarmed! It was over a month after joining that I took my first solo in the Mk 5 Vampire. Luckily someone had casually mentioned that on finals the stick on the Vampire appeared to go dead as full flap was lowered but I was still not prepared for it. I had to ram the stick right forward to prevent stalling and retrim hard. Another little peculiarity of the Vampire was the high speed stall in very tight turns - very quirky habit as it just flicked out when the G forces got too high and you ended up a long way from the flight path.

Something I found odd about security on this master airfield was the fact that the Coca-cola lorry was allowed to visit the crewroom and restock our private fridge which served as the drinks cabinet.

In the middle of May, I with the junior pilots of 5 and 11 squadrons were sent on an aerial gunnery course at RAF Sylt, Westerland. An idyllic posting up in the Freisian Islands, it was a very popular beach resort for the German civilians and of course we spent all our off-duty time in the sand dunes. It was also famous for the "Abessinien" nude bathing beach where, more precisely, we spent all our time. I have a great poster advertising the resort. Anyone caught low flying over the beach was disciplined.

The air-to air exercises consisted of firing at a drogue towed behind a Tempest. This was the last of the long line of piston-engined fighters - a beautiful but massive and powerful beast. They were piloted usually by people on minor disciplinary charges, but also by the station CO. Towing was a bit of a hairy occupation because the pilot could be shot up if the attacker got the angle wrong or, if the drop release did not work, the aircraft had to land with the flag still attached to a long cable. There were possible dire consequences if the flag caught on anything coming over the hedge. It was also extremely boring for the towing pilot just flying set legs up and down the target area over the North Sea. On two or three occasions the log book records "abort" which indicates that the flag had been shot away between taking off and locating the tug and the Tempest was returning to base. On one of these days, rather than waste the flight I decided to have a look around and set off in a northerly direction. It was not long before I found 2 light blue coloured Meteors of the Danish airforce alongside me and signalling to go back! The boundary of Denmark was just along the north beach of the island.

Three or four incidents I recall from the flying side brought home the dangers of the job. One was a collision while firing on the flag. The attack on the drogue was done with pairs of aircraft attacking alternately and calling "clear" for the next chap to go in. I do not know what went wrong but two from No 5 collided with the nose of one Vampire rammed between the twin booms of the other. They managed to separate and land safely but one had its booms bent at quite an angle!

Another time was on the ground and fatal. Aircraft have an air/ground switch which is always switched to ground once the turbine has been closed down.
One pilot, not one of the Wunstorf contingent, climbed in to start up after the armourers had reloaded the canon shells and switched to "air" as normal to start up and the canons started firing on their own. Unfortunately a member of the groundcrew was in the line of fire. I do not know what the enquiry concluded on the incident.

Another incident involved me because I was due to fly and on my pre-flight inspection noticed marked corrugations in the wings. The Engineering Officer was called and concluded that someone must have made a heavy landing and not reported it and the machine was wheeled away. Luckily, I had noticed as I was a bit cavalier about things and usually just jumped in and went.

I was a compulsive helmet jack swinger when

walking away from an aircraft and had been told about it. In every crewroom was a device to check that the radio connections on the helmet were working properly and I did my checks regularly. For some reason, I was to fly this sortie on my own and not as a pair but the weather was not very good with lots of low level cloud around and I just could not locate the target tug with the CO who was flying the Tempest that day. Worse, my R/T kept breaking up and I could not make out his instructions so I reported returning to base. As I had been above cloud for some time trying to find him I had no idea where I was rather relying on picking up the Tempest for a location. I could not remember which ways I had turned and for how long so I was lost. I called the tower for directions - nothing. Several attempts produced the same result. I could still not see the ground and had enough fuel for 15 -20 minutes. Thinking hard I concluded that I might be way out over the North Sea, in which case I could safely let down over the sea or, more likely I was way south (not north because the Danes had not reappeared!). We always flew with the local map (which I still have with several others covering the continent) tucked in our boot so I tried to hazard a guess on position from it when a fleeting break in the cloud occurred and I had a momentary glimpse of a small island. It looked like something I could identify on the map as Blauortand about 55 miles away so set off on an estimated course home. Broken cloud over Westerland proved my guess to be right and with a waggle of wings past the tower to indicate no R/T I joined the circuit to land after a maximum possible flight of

45 minutes.

We had on base a Sri Lankan pilot who had painted his Vampire with a lurid shark's mouth on the lower part of the nose. It was said that he was such a heavy handed pilot that all his control cables had been made loose for him so much that no one else could fly the machine!

One of our squadron also narrowly avoided a collision in one bizarre happening. He was having an affair with a WAAF officer at the time and arrived one morning with little sleep. It is said he dozed off while attacking the flag and snagged his wing on the cable - the aircraft had a fixed slot on the leading wing which had caught up under the towing cable and sent him sliding along it. Luckily he wrenched it off and broke away before crashing into the tail of the towing aircraft.

During our stay here Queen Elizabeth II's Coronation took place and the Officers' Mess had hired in a television and invited all the local civilian dignitaries to attend a cocktail party to watch and celebrate the occasion. The t/v reception was not brilliant but snowy pictures were often the norm in the early days of television. One of the German party got legless before the actual crowning and the rest of his party wedged him in the corner and stood round him to stop him falling over!

It was a great fun time and our beach exploits must await the telling at another time. But there was one sad moment in all the madcap activities on the station. A welsh auxiliary squadron came to train alongside us and they were a devil-may-care partying crowd. One night they returned from town in the dark in two vehicles. Use of the runways by vehicles was permitted once flying had ceased for the day. Each one sped down a runway only to collide at the intersection and 2 were killed.

All too soon our 3-week holiday was over during which I had added 10 hours on 18 flights plus gained a lot of handling experience and it was time to take the train home. Back at Wunsdorf the handling trials were over, gun stoppages that had been a problem were rectified and some new Venoms had arrived so I could be fully integrated into squadron activities. It had taken nearly 2 1/2 months from reporting for duty. After a quick dual check (I was still able to claim it as second pilot) on the Meteor, as no dual trainer of the Venom had been produced, I was handed the keys to a Venom for my first flight. It was lovely to fly and had quite different handling techniques to the Vampire. It was about this time that relations with the Russians deteriorated further and orders came through for us to fly fully armed and the rules of engagement were established. It meant that if we were attacked we could engage if we had a first class fix to establish that we were not violating Russian airspace (and hope to stay alive whilst transmitting and awaiting the reply!). I mainly flew one of the originally delivered airplanes which meant that we were supposed to observe the restricted mach and G limitations. They were identified by a red stripe across each wing.   Another drawback with these early machines was that they had no ejector seat so there would not be much chance of exiting at any speed.   None of the squadron were getting much flying in during this time of re-equiping because the new aircraft were subject to a 50-hour engine change which meant that one or two were always out of action.

One of the hazards of flying, but an unexpected one, was reported in the monthly flying accident reports which, presumably, the two NS pilots we had left behind at headquarters were now publishing. As operational pilots we might have to fly over water. We therefore had to allow for emergency ditching or baling out over the sea. Consequently we always flew wearing life jackets and our parachute packs included a one-man inflatable dinghy which had a gas bottle to inflate it and I cannot remember whether it automatically inflated on hitting the water or a lever on the gas bottle had to be pulled when you were in the water. One report was of a pilot who perished when at height his dinghy self inflated filling the cockpit so that the stick was pushed forward and the pinioned pilot could not use the controls. To counteract the possibility it was recommended that we flew with an accessible small sheath knife (not provided!). Mine is preserved somewhere and was worn tied to the front of the life jacket. The recommended method of destruction was repeated stabbing between the legs – taking great care to keep personal parts out of the way!

Wunstorf was a very comfortable station, the

more so because of a lovely retreat at the lakeside of the Steinhudermere. This was the Officers' Mess annexe, fully equipped with bar and all facilities including our own sailing club. It was fun to take the boats out and I quickly picked up the rudiments of handling sail, but what the class of boat was I cannot recall other than they were 14 footers. I was warned by the more experienced among my fellow officers that the waters could get a little tricky because of phenomena known as a "Steinhuder Special", a strong wind which could spring up from nowhere: but I was never caught in one. The annexe also has an unofficial Mercedes car used to transport us - said to have been taken from a German officer during the Allied advance and kept on the station ever since. We used the place as a weekend club and spent a lot of time there when not visiting Hannover.

We made frequent visits into Hannover where there was a good Officers' Club. On one occasion at night, three of us had diverted down some narrow sidestreets to be confronted by a gang of youths who started to come towards us singing the old German marching songs so we reversed pretty quickly. On another occasion I was returning to the airfield, very late after an amorous visit to the village, and had taken the short cut along the narrow back road which went for a mile or two between fields without any habitation - completely deserted of all people and traffic. Quite suddenly a man lurched out from behind a tree and shouted something in German. I did not stop to find out what he wanted but took to my heels and he gave chase!

It was a long one but I was obviously the fitter of us but I was relieved to see the guardhouse appearing and, as it was not a main entrance, hoped it was still manned at the late hour. It was and I lived to tell the tale!

In less than a week of my first Venom flight another diversion took place in that the whole squadron was posted to RAF Wattisham with orders to take part in the Coronation Review over Odiham to celebrate the accession of Queen Elizabeth II.

We received our sealed orders for what was quite a detailed enterprise a day or two before departure. At this time I had caught the eye of a young lady - with who I later became very involved - but at this time anxious not to let her get away I asked her to write down her name for me. Searching my pockets the only paper I had were my secret orders - which somehow still survive among my papers - so her handwriting can be seen on them. Only senior pilots flew aircraft across to England and I and two other pilots each took charge of one third of the large party of men going by train and boat which was good practice in shepherding, feeding and quartering a large group. I cannot remember if we lost anyone but we ran into difficulties at HM Customs at The Hook. One of the ground crew had a new and empty camera case in his possession and Customs wanted to know where the camera was. The clot had hidden it on one of the aircraft coming over so we telephoned Wunstorf to tell them to expect trouble. Each aircraft was searched and lots of contraband found hidden behind the panels. It was a highly dangerous thing to do without telling the pilot because aircraft performance might have been affected. Whilst on the subject, the aircraft taken to the UK were still obliged to return to Germany for the engine changes. Each time they returned juicy steaks, unheard of in austerity Britain, were brought back for our mess dinners - probably carried in the same nooks and crannies of the aircraft for the same reason!

Early on in my days at Wattisham, when supposed to be doing a local recce, I thought it would be nice to fly over Mum's house in Patcham. It took about 7 minutes and I went over quite low and straight out to sea and then kept low all the way back round Kent at sea level in case anyone had taken my number!
None of us had a chance to fly a lot from Wattisham because of the small number of aircraft flown over and there were more pilots than machines. One was written off while there. The Wing Commander had taken delivery of a brand new one with smart black & white chequered motif along the fuselage. We were watching him take off on one of the practice formations when, he claimed, something went wrong with the engine and he pulled his undercarriage up and skidded on the aircraft's belly and into the grass at the end of the runway.

Flying the Coronation Review was a tiring business as we flew in boxes of 4 with our tip tanks in line and a short distance apart. It was quite a sight when all the other squadrons of different types were in line astern. Among my surviving records is the map marked with our flight path from Wattisham to the west of London and over Odiham then east over East Grinstead and Tunbridge Wells and then north to the east of London back to base. Incidentally, at the time of writing this map could be of historical interest as it shows the position of airfields in 1951. They are fast disappearing as a recent visit to Stoney Cross in the New Forest showed as we could see no signs of one near the Travelodge.

To speed up the return of the ground party to Wunstorf when the grand event was over, Transport Command was enlisted and we, with all our stores and equipment, were flown back in a Valetta. It took 2 hours instead of 2 days.
In view of the gap between my last Venom flight in England and the return to Wunstorf I must have gone home on leave. It was about this time that I had the sad news that one of my old school chums Pete Philips had been killed in a flying accident at OCU Stradishall. OCU is an Operational Conversion Unit, the last stage of training before joining a squadron and the stage that was cut out for me.

I remember one sad occasion at a Sunday lunch time, when officers and wives met in the bar for pre-lunch drinks, news came through that someone with 266 squadron was returning from a routine battle flight on fire. He was just over the runway when his rudder cables burnt through.

What turned out to be my last day of flying with No.11 occurred 2 days after return. It was the

Dutch Airforce's 40th anniversary and we were booked at the weekend for a commemoration flypast at Soesterberg. I was nominated as reserve and took off with the 4 others on what was supposed to be a short daytime excursion - back for lunch. Consequently, I was flying the only aircraft available, still in charge of the maintenance unit, but cleared only for daylight flying as the navigation lights were missing and deficiency chits were inserted in the covers where lights should have been. We had expected a quick touchdown, refuel, on to the flypast and then home but it did not work out that way. As we landed a mother of a storm blew up and we were grounded for several hours. Not expecting to have to stay for hospitality at the host airfield at RAF Wildenrath on the Dutch border I had flown in flying suit over trousers and a collarless shirt so had to borrow a collar and tie to get into the mess. Eventually we were cleared to fly but only at low level because of the black cloud base. Flt Lt Bob Tanner was leading our flight and when they taxied out I saw, too late to join them immediately, that a colleague had failed to start. I had to allow a contingent of Meteors to take off before I could get after them and went like a bat out of hell to catch them and reported that I was in the box. Then my red warning light came on and stayed on, which usually meant serious engine trouble. I reported to Bob who told me to break off and try to get back to Wildenrath, which I did. Back on the ground, the small ground crew who had joined us by road ran up the engine and could find nothing wrong. After the formation returned from the flypast it was decided that I should try to take off and nurse the aircraft back to Wunstorf where full facilities were available. It was getting dark and as I had no navigation lights I went back in formation with Bob but the red warning light came on and stayed on. By the end we were night flying and I discovered that as well as having no nav. lights I had no cockpit lights either which was not a problem while in formation because Bob was doing the necessary. However when we broke for finals I had no way of seeing the airspeed. Fortunately, I was a smoker in those days and was able to light my gas lighter to illuminate the dial. To commemorate the event the Dutch airforce awarded gongs but I did not get one. We subsequently heard that because of the low cloud base someone doing aerobatics at the show had ploughed in. By coincidence, while writing this memoir (Feb '06), I received the Corgi model catalogue and listed in it is a model of an RNAF Meteor that flew in their aerobatic team at Soesterberg.

It was many years later when working for National Savings in East Anglia that the senior voluntary worker told me a very sad tale. His son had been killed when flying with the Royal Navy. His machine had the same engine as the Venom and at the enquiry it was ascertained that while flying over the Irish Sea his red light had come on and, as the standard procedure was to bale out immediately, he had done so. Unfortunately, he could not be picked up before hypothermia caused death. I cannot now remember how the matter came up and I had been relating how I had trouble on that flight back from Soesterberg but got back to base. He went very quiet and I could have bitten my tongue because I had no idea that his son had been killed in a flying accident, nor that the circumstances had been the same as mine. Food for thought because either my aircraft might have blown up or, if his son had kept flying he would have lived to tell the tale.

Shortly after the Soesterberg event my affair with 11 Squadron ended rather abruptly. At some time previously we had had 2 VIP visits involving full dress parades to receive them. The first was from the Chief of Air Staff, Lord De L'Isle, who enquired if I would be staying on in the Royal Air Force. When I started to explain my position, the Squadron CO cut me short with "he is adamant that he will not be" and the parade party moved on. Some time after, I have just found on internet that the date was 19 April, the Duke of Edinburgh visited but this time he was hurried past me before any question could be asked. The position arose because, earlier, I had been asked to sign on a short service commission but declined unless I was offered a permanent commission. The squadron was now fully equipped with Venoms and wanted to ensure that they had a full team for the forseeable future - a perfectly understandable position. On the other hand I knew how perfidious governments could be and that their persuasive argument that if I signed on for 4 years, I would be put up for a permanent commission, did not wash. I responded, either do it now or forget it. My reasons were that if pilots were no longer wanted at the end of the 4 years - and the services have a long history of rapid expansion or equally rapid reduction - I might have difficulty getting a job in civvy street whereas I now had a guaranteed job to go back to. On top of that I knew that I would retain my commission and continue flying in the flying club-like atmosphere of the RAFVR for another 4 years and probably longer - but even that was not to be as I have recorded later. Carter did sign on and so did my old mates from the Airspeed Oxford days, Tony Sumner and Mike Neal, who signed on for 12 years. In the event, if I had done the same, 1965 would have been the year of discharge and it proved to be a boom year with jobs aplenty and a £15000 gratuity would have been mine. At that time houses could be bought for £2-3000 or less and the gratuity would have started a good self-employed business with opportunities abounding - instead we had struggled to save enough to get married and still had a 90% mortgage on a £1995 bungalow - cette-la vie.

And so 4 days after returning to Wunstorf from the excursion to Wattisham I found myself travelling to Oldenburg with a permanent posting to 26 squadron. Another internet excursion has uncovered an account of another pilot joining 11 Squadron and, although I have only vague recollection of him either on 11, or 5 to which he says he was transferred. I thought it rather a snobbish account of an officer with a permanent commission who seemed to dismiss the national service pilots. However, it is interesting to compare his account with my experiences, that for both of us tactical training was skipped for the expediency of getting us into the front line, particularly the fact that the squadron also had to teach him to fly jets.

Chapter Thirteen

26 Squadron

I had landed with an old Vampire Squadron with less than a month to go before the demobilisation processes started to run. It was a very casual almost rag-bag outfit, actually a South African squadron but no signs of any great affiliation with that country. One of the newly joined pilots had just returned from flying Meteors in Korea. My only memories are of readings from "The Perfumed Garden" by the CO in the crewroom and the mad telephone answering dares - chalked up were responses we had to make to callers no matter who they were and we had to take it in turns. At some weekends I returned by train to Wunsdorf until reluctant goodbyes before the final journey home.

It was at one weekend that I returned to what might have been serious trouble. That Saturday morning I was up flying alone when some other squadron members found me and in attempts to shake them off I had done one or two bunts - negative G manoeuvres that bring the blood into the eyes if not careful. After landing I went off for the weekend and on Monday an inspection of the aircraft revealed acid had eaten into the main spar due to battery spillage. Flying Standing Orders were looked up to prove that all negative G flying had to be reported on landing and as I had not done so and had been seen by the other pilots my butt was on the line! My luck held because when the book of Orders that I had signed was turned up this particular order was missing and I could claim not to have known about it! Subsequently, an aircraft fitter admitted that he had not put the battery caps back on so he was on a charge instead. I have also found on internet that 3 months after I left the squadron was re-equipped with Sabres.

I left Germany on 19th August, just 1 year, 11months and 22 days after that apprehensive train ride to RAF Padgate.

There are some momentos of my days in Germany including my concessionary rail pass, some BAFs (funny money used within the Services), some stamps left over from writing home and an aircraft recognition leaflet acquired at some period of training on the squadron plus the maps and a navigation ruler.

Chapter Fourteen

Demob

RAF Innsworth , actually No.1 Personal Holding Unit, was my home until 27 August, thus completing exactly the 2 years commitment to National Service. They were depressing days signing off, handing in bits of uniform and flying gear and I wondered if I had made the right choice. All that I was left with were my helmet with oxygen mask attached, a battledress, 2 shirts and a tie, a beret and my officer's raincoat. Everthing else was handed in. I cannot remember being given the VR badges for my lapels and I think I had to pay for them. With an excess of zeal I was obliged to sign the Official Secrets Acts again - signed on 21.08.53. Bereft of rank and privilege, I cashed in my rail warrant and travelled back to Brighton via Paddington.

Typically, my termination of service letter, which also granted 24 days terminal leave, was dated 21 October, exactly 1 month after the leave expired!

Most of my memorabilia items were kept at home to where they had been addressed but I did leave Innsworth with a collection of maps and one or two other items used in flying.

Chapter Fifteen

Reserve Flying School

My official letter of appointment to the RAFVR is dated 29 October, 1953 and the rules in a follow-up letter of 13 November, 1953.

Now officially on the Reserve, I joined No 15 RFS at Redhill where we flew Chipmunks from the grass airfield on Nutfield Ridge. Happy days but all too short. The arrangement was that I could fly anytime on a casual basis if the unit had availability in addition to an annual 2-weeks full time commitment. I cannot remember why there was a delay but I had a day's flying in January and turned up for my 2 weeks in March to find that at the end the RAFVR was being disbanded as part of the Government's economy drive. During that fortnight 3 things stand out in my memory. The first on 10th March when, on a cross country to Thorney Island, I saw one of the prototype Saunders Roe Princesses flying up the Solent and flew alongside it. A beautiful aircraft with 10 engines, largest flying boat ever made but it proved to be a Do-Do among the current land based passenger aircraft coming off the drawing board. It was on one of the last flights it made. Jeremy Clarkson has written about this aircraft in his book "I Know You Got Soul", p43. Second, 3 of us flew for the last time on a massive cross country, with 2 refuelling stops, a total of 4 hours in formation all the way with an ex-Battle of Britain pilot leading. Finally, on our last night all the VR pilots were invited to drink the bar dry for free as all the accumulated stocks had to go. I spent most of the evening with Connie who had some connection with another VR chap - it got hazy as the evening progressed. She was foolish enough to give her car keys to someone who pranged the car. Luckily I still had a bed on the camp to tumble into after a heavy night.

And so my RAF days ended as they had mostly been spent. At least I still have my chit authorising me to draw flying kit!

All the records I have from those last days of flying in the VR are "Notes on Chipmunk Handling" and a blank compass swinging form.

The final accolade came just as everything folded up - my substantive promotion to Flying Officer. On a typically scrappy piece of paper from the Air Ministry the Gazette Supplement extract shows a date of 9 June 1954 - a late birthday present

Chapter Sixteen

Disbandment of the Royal Air Force Volunteer Reserve

Notification of closure of the VR stations as an economy measure is given in a lengthy document accompanying a letter of 21 April, 1954 from HQ. Although the letter stated that I would be eligible to train at an operating RAF station in view of my recent experience on modern operational aircraft the call never came and perhaps the financial constraint of having to pay a bounty (para 15) if I was became the deciding factor.

The final letter dated 25 May 1956 confirmed that any hope of more flying at the public expense was dead but Air Ministry letter 17.01.57 informed me of liability to recall after disbandment.

A slim chance resurrected itself in January 1957 when, no doubt due to yet another lurch in the cold war, my obligation to serve was extended to June 1959.

Almost as a postscipt to my Air Force service came the last time I wore uniform. It was nothing to do with any unit and as we were now officially disbanded probably I no longer entitled to wear it. It was the occasion of my old poser friend Norman's marriage (long time annulled) to Celia. Norman asked me to be Best Man – in uniform of course.

After 2 years full time service and just over 6 months on the reserve I ended with the following score of hours at the controls:

Tiger Moth	12
Chipmunk	88*
Oxford	131
Meteor	76
Vampire	29
Venom	10

	366
	===

*excluding civilian flights

Epilogue

Chapter Seventeen

Flying in later years.

The coincidence surrounding Flt/Sgt Smith (see days at Holme-on-Spalding-Moor) happened when my old friend Brian Loosley (who died aged 39) and I went on holiday to Jersey and flew from Shoreham in a DeHavilland Dove. One of us, as last to board, had to sit up front with the pilot as the aircraft was overbooked and I was chosen being the lighter of the two of us. Imagine both our surprise when passenger and pilot recognised each other from days flying Oxfords. When airbourne we chatted and I told him that I eventually got to a fighter squadron and he said he would have expected it. Then he said he had a lot of paperwork to do so left me looking out with a hand on the controls!

As a birthday present in 1990 my children booked me a flying lesson in a Cessna C150. It was a culture shock after a lapse of 46 years at the controls but surprisingly so much came back and we had a lot of fun in the local area, including low flying (but at a legal height not my 5 feet above ground in my old lawless days). My confidence went right up when I was allowed to fly the approach and land. My next flight in 1998 was wangled for me by my son-in-law James who at the time was reporting from an airborne position on traffic congestion for his local radio station and had a spare seat in his Piper PA28. The pilot let me do most of the flying and it included a memorable flight in glorious sunshine parallel to the tops of the white Seven Sisters chalk cliffs of East Sussex to Brighton and again I did the landing. But a very special reunion came later that year as a 65th birthday present when the children booked me for a Chipmunk flight. This was a special aircraft based at Shoreham with dispensation to fly in RAF markings. Some things were not the same because we had to sit with cushions in the seat well rather than a parachute and the cartridge starter had been replaced by a car starter motor. Unfortunately the weather on 5 June was far from ideal and after about 30 minutes in rather claggy weather Mike Hurlihy suggested we called it a day and he would arrange a credit for the remaining 1/2 hour. I nearly lost the credit because of a combination of circumstances involving us not being able to get up from Somerset and reorganisation of the flying school under new management who considered the credit to be time expired. However, eventually the school relented and we came up to Sussex on the momentous but very anxious day of 26 June 1999 because we were expecting to hear of the birth of our first grandchild. The news of David Austin's arrival came through a few minutes before we walked out to start up and I was able to do a victory roll just east of Arundel. My flying career ended on this day because I had the good sense to realise that at 66 it was time to leave it to the younger men. But it was a fantastic way to go out, 48 years after I first climbed into a cockpit with the chance to leave the ground and just under 48 years since my first flight in a Chipmunk.

The nearest I have been to it since was being invited into the jump seat up front of a DC10 on the take-off from Dubai to Hong Kong (daughter Kate being on duty with cabin crew of British Caledonian on that trip) and much later a flight to the Scillies from Lands End.

Between 1979 and 1987 I travelled many hundreds of miles on passenger aircraft to the Americas, Caribbean and the continent on Government business.

Chapter Eighteen

And Flying Related Matters

I came across a reference to the re-equipping of 11 Squadron with Venoms in the cutting of an obit for David Leech. I think the author got his facts wrong because if Leech joined in 1954 he could not have got to operational flying in less than a year's training - and it seems he was moved on pretty quickly too.

A club related to the services was the Victory Services Club in Seymour Street W2. Its virtues were extolled by the many of the retired regular officers serving under me as District Commissioners in my National Savings days at Cambridge as a convenient and cheap place for accommodation in London. It was OK on price but depended on getting a room in the new wing with facilities because the old wing was without. It came in useful in between changing jobs from Cambridge to London and our family move to Haywards Heath. Membership lapsed with approaching retirement as I did not expect to have any further need for it.

After my demob one of Norman's birthday presents to me was enrolment in the Brevet Flying Club. Strictly for aircrew, it had premises in the prestigious area of Chesterfield Street W1, with bar and overnight accommodation but was a bit scruffy. Membership cards were in the form of the then current driving licence adapted to a drinking licence and I kept it going for 7 years after which I think the Club folded but not before I had both popped in for the odd drink and on one occasion stayed there.

I lost touch with my old friends from the aircrew training days. I received Christmas cards from Tony Sumner, who had signed on, and learned that he was married and had 2 boys. 2 of the cards survive to show that he was first an instructor at the Operational Conversion Unit at Pembrey and later at Chivenor. Geoff Rothon I saw a few times when he visited me in Patcham, first on his new Velocette and later in his new MGTF. Of all the ones who wanted to make a career in flying, as he had done so much as an Air Cadet, he had the worst deal as on qualifying he was made adjutant of a Reserve Unit in Kent and left the RAF after his 2 years to go back into banking.

Chapter Nineteen

Conclusion.

So my enforced service to my country turned out to be a unique, exciting and, in the end, a comfortable way of life. As Michael Caine, who is a National Service contemporary but who served in Korea, says in his memoirs, it made a man of him and so it did me too. I think I had enormous luck, not just in avoiding accidents but in getting through a most exacting training. Of all the NS chaps who had enrolled to be aircrew, I was one of the very few who survived the course to fly on a squadron.

Printed in Great Britain
by Amazon